180 SOLVED CASES IN DAX LANGUAGE

POWER BI

Business Intelligence

Ramón J. Castro

Revised edition by Irene Castro Miranda

©Publicaciones Rebel Out Post
©180 SOLVED CASES IN DAX LANGUAGE

First edition (2021)

©Author:: Ramón Javier Castro Amador (2021)
©Cover designed by Ramón Javier Castro Amador (2021)

Copyright: 2109089203819
Web: www.facebook.com/180casosresueltosenlenguajedax
Email: publicaciones.rebel.out.post@gmail.com

We don't know when it will rain or how much it will fall, but when it does, we know where it will pass.

Index

Introduction

This book is intended as a quick guide that compiles a total of 180 common DAX language case studies for quick resolution. All the DAX code collected in the book can be tested through the file:

180_Casos_Resueltos_en_Lenguaje_DAX.pbix

accessible for download:

www.facebook.com/180casosresueltosenlenguajedax

180 Solved Cases in Dax Language is the first of four quick guides to solving cases in DAX language. The other titles are:

- 90 Solved Cases on Time Intelligence in Dax
- 80 Solved Cases on Statistics in Dax
- 60 Solved Cases on Finance in Dax

Solved Cases

001. Create CALENDAR table
Table tools > new table

```
Calendar =
ADDCOLUMNS (
        //start_date, end_date
        CALENDAR ( MIN ( Sales[Date] ), TODAY () ),
        //numerical values
        "year", YEAR ( [Date] ),
        "month", MONTH ( [Date] ),
        "day", DAY ( [Date] ),
        "quarter", QUARTER ( [Date] ),
        "weekDay", WEEKDAY ( [Date] ),
        "weekNum", WEEKNUM ( [Date] ),
        // text values
        "monthName", FORMAT ( [Date], "MMM" ),
        "weekDayName", FORMAT ( [Date], "DDD" ),
        "quarterName", SWITCH ( QUARTER ( [Date] ), 1,
"First", 2, "Second", 3, "Third", 4, "quarter")
)
```

002. Create blank table
Table tools > new table

```
Customer Complaints =
//create a table and insert data
//column name , field type (INTEGER, DOUBLE, STRING,
BOOLEAN, CURRENCY, DATETIME)
DATATABLE (
        "Country", STRING,
        "Complaints", INTEGER,
        "Year", DATETIME,
```

//introduction of data in the fields following the previous order

```
{
{ "Canada", 32, 2014 },
{ "Germany", 26, 2014 },
{ "France", 42, 2014 },
{ "Mexico", 18, 2014 },
{ "USA", 38, 2014 },
{ "Canada", 12, 2015 },
{ "Germany", 32, 2015 },
{ "France", 24, 2015 },
{ "Mexico", 30, 2015 },
{ "USA", 27, 2015 },
{ "Canada", 23, 2016 },
{ "Germany", 24, 2016 },
{ "France", 36, 2016 },
{ "Mexico", 27, 2016 },
{ "USA", 32, 2016 }
}
)
```

003. Create a table with unique values from one column
Table tools > new table

Fields with unique values =
//over a column
DISTINCT(Sales[Country])

004. Creating a table with unique rows from a table
Table tools > new table

Rows with unique values =
//over a table returns unique rows
DISTINCT(Sales)

005. Create calculate table (1)

Table tools > new table

Total and Subtotal per category (1) =
//create a table that groups subtotals by categories
SUMMARIZE(
    //source table
    Sales,
    //column to group by
    ROLLUP(Sales[Contry]),
    //calculated expressions
    "Sum", SUM(Sales[Sales]),
    "Avg", AVERAGE(Sales[Sales])
)

006. Create calculate table (2)

Table tools > new table

Total and Subtotal per category (2) =
//create a table that groups subtotals by category from
more than one filter
SUMMARIZE(
    //source table
    CALCULATETABLE(
        //source table
        Sales,
        //applying filters to the resulting table
        FILTER(Sales, Sales[Sales]>10000),
        FILTER(Sector,
    Sector[Sector]="Midmarket")
    ),
    //column to group by
    ROLLUP(Sales[Country]),
    //calculated expressions
    "Sum", SUM(Sales[Sales]),
    "Avg", AVERAGE(Sales[Sales])

)

007. Create calculate table (3)

Table tools > new table

```
Total and Subtotal per category (3) =
//create a table that groups subtotals by categories
SUMMARIZE(
        //source table
        SUMMARIZE(
                //source table
                Sales,
                //resulting table
                Sales[Country],
                Calendar[Year],
                Sales[ Sales]
        ),
        //column to group by
        ROLLUP('Calendar'[year]),
        //calculated expressions
        "Sum", SUM(Sales[ Sales]),
        "Avg", AVERAGE(Sales[ Sales])
)
```


008. Create calculate table (4)

Table tools > new table

```
Total and Subtotal per >1 category (4) =
//create a table that groups subtotals by several
categories
ADDCOLUMNS(
        //source table
        SUMMARIZE(
                //source table.
                Sales,
```

```
            //column to group by
            Sales[Country],
            Calendar[Year]
    ),
    //calculated expressions
    "Sum", CALCULATE(SUM(Sales[ Sales])),
    "Avg", CALCULATE(AVERAGE(Sales[ Sales]))
)
```

009. Create calculate table (5)
Table tools > new table

```
Sales on 2016 =
//create a table that meets a condition
CALCULATETABLE(
        //source table
        Sales ,
        //filter
        'Calendar'[year] = 2016
)
```

010. Create calculate table (6)
Table tools > new table

```
Sales on Canada 2016 =
//create a table that meets more than one condition
CALCULATETABLE (
        //source table
        Sales,
        //filters
        Sales[Country] = "Canada",
        'Calendar'[year] = 2016
)
```

011. Create calculate table (7)

Table tools > new table

Sales to salesman per sector =
//create a table by selecting columns from another table
SELECTCOLUMNS (
        //source table
        Sales,
        //name new columns, column data source
        "salesman", Sales[Salesman],
        "sector", Sales[Sector],
        "totalSales", SUM (Sales[Sales])
)

012. Create calculate table (8)

Table tools > new table

Sales to salesman per sector =
//create a table by selecting columns from TWO tables or more
//unrelated tables
SELECTCOLUMNS (
        //source table
        Sales,
        //name new columns, column data source
        "country", Sales[Country],
        "tax", LOOKUPVALUE (
                //value to extract
                'Country Tax'[Tax],
                //search column
                'Country Tax'[Country],
                //column from which to extract
        the value to search for
                [Country]
        ),
        "totalSales", SUM (Sales[Sales])

7

)

013. Create calculate table (9)

Table tools > new table

Sales per country (1) =
//create a calculated table with the sales summary by country
SUMMARIZECOLUMNS (
    //table and columns
    Sales[country],
    //new column, expression
    "totalSales", SUM (Sales[Sales]),
    "Average Sales", AVERAGEX('Sales', SUM (Sales[Sales])),
    "Max Sales", MAXX('Sales', SUM (Sales[Sales])),
    "Min Sales", MINX('Sales', SUM (Sales[Sales])),
    "Sales Count", COUNTROWS('Sales')
)

014. Create calculate table (10)

Table tools > new table

Sales to sector per country (2) =
//create a calculated table with the sales summary by country, filtering by a value from the same table
SUMMARIZECOLUMNS (
    //table and columns
    Sales[country],
    //filter
    FILTER (Sales, Sales[Sector] = "Government"),
    //calculated columns
    "totalSales", SUM (Sales[Sales]),
    "Average Sales", AVERAGEX('Sales', SUM (Sales[Sales])),

8

```
        "Max Sales", MAXX('Sales', SUM ( Sales[ Sales] ) ),
        "Min Sales", MINX('Sales', SUM ( Sales[ Sales] ) ),
        "Sales Count", COUNTROWS('Sales')
)
```

015. Create calculate table (11)
Table tools > new table

```
Sales to Government sector per country in 2015 =
//create a calculated table with the sales summary by
country, filtering by a value from another related table
SUMMARIZECOLUMNS (
        //table and columns
        Sales[country],
        //filters
        FILTER ( Sector, Sector[Sector] = "Government" ),
        FILTER ( 'Calendar', 'Calendar'[year] = 2015),
        //calculated columns
        "totalSales", SUM ( Sales[ Sales] ),
        "Average Sales", AVERAGEX('Sales', SUM ( Sales[
Sales] ) ),
        "Max Sales", MAXX('Sales', SUM ( Sales[ Sales] ) ),
        "Min Sales", MINX('Sales', SUM ( Sales[ Sales] ) ),
        "Sales Count", COUNTROWS('Sales')
)
```

016. Create calculate table (12)
Table tools > new table

```
Average sales amount per seller =
//create a table grouped by a condition
SELECTCOLUMNS (
        //table
        Salesman,
        //new columns
```

9

```
        "Name", Salesman[Salesman],
        "Gender", Salesman[Gender],
        //RELATEDTABLE evaluates a table expression in a
context modified by the specified filters
        //relationship type from "many" to "one".
        "Average sales", AVERAGEX ( RELATEDTABLE (
Sales ), Sales[ Sales] )
)
```

017. Create calculate table (13)
Table tools > new table

```
Average sales amount per seller and gender M =
//create a table grouped by more than one condition
SELECTCOLUMNS (
        FILTER ( Salesman, Salesman[Gender] = "M" ),
        "Name", Salesman[Salesman],
        "Gender", Salesman[Gender],
        //RELATEDTABLE evaluates a table expression in a
context modified by the specified filters
        //relationship type: from "many" to "one"
        "Average sales", AVERAGEX ( RELATEDTABLE (
Sales ), Sales[ Sales] )
)
```

018. Create calculate table (14)
Table tools > new table

```
Total and Subtotal per >1 category (5) =
//create a table that groups subtotals by various
categories from one or more filters
FILTER(
        ADDCOLUMNS(
                SUMMARIZE(
                        //source table
```

```
            Sales,
            //column to group by
            Sales[Country],
            Calendar[Year]
        ),
        //calculated expressions
        "Sum", SUM(Sales[ Sales]),
        "Avg", AVERAGE(Sales[ Sales])
    ),
    //use columns of the resulting table as a filter
    AND( [Sum] > 5000000, Sales[Country]="USA")
)
```

019. Create single row calculated table
Table tools > new table

```
Total sales =
//create a single-row table showing the values obtained
from an expression
ROW (
        //column name, expression
        "Total sales", SUM ( Sales[ sales] ),
        "Total COGS", SUM ( Sales[COGS])
)
```

020. Create table with single values from another table
Table tools > new table

```
Countries with sales =
//select table
//get rows with unique values
VALUES(Sales)
```

021. Create table with unique values from a column contained in another table

Table tools > new table

Countries with sales =
//select table[column]
//get column with unique values
VALUES(Sales[contry])

022. Add a column from a table to another table

Table tools > new column

Add province to sales =
//related tables
//create a new column in table Sales
RELATED(Country[Province])

023. Append a column from a table to another table if it meets a condition (1)

Table tools > new column

Sales in Niza =
//related tables
//create a new column in table Sales
//meet one condition
IF(
        Sales[Country]="France",
        RELATED(Country[Province]),
        BLANK()
)

024. Add a column from a table to another table if it meets more than one condition (2)

Table tools > new column

```
Sales in Niza in 2016 =
//related tables
//create a new column in table Sales
//meets more than one condition
IF(
        AND( Sales[Country]="France", Sales[Date]=2016
),
        RELATED(Country[Province]),
        BLANK()
)
```

025. Add a column from an unrelated table to another table

Table tools > new column

```
Tax by sale (4) =
//unrelated tables
//create a new column in table Sales
//the tax data is taken from the Country Tax table
LOOKUPVALUE(
        //value to extract
        'Country Tax'[Tax],
        //search column
        'Country Tax'[Country],
        //column from which to extract the value to
search for
        Sales[Country]
)
```

13

026. Add a column from a table to another table if it satisfies more than one condition (1)
Table tools > new column

Tax by sale in Germany (5) =
//unrelated tables
//create a new column in table Sales
//the tax data is taken from the Country Tax table
//one condition must be met
IF(

     Country2[Country] = "Germany",

     LOOKUPVALUE(

          //value to extract

          'Country Tax'[Tax],

          //search column

          'Country Tax'[Country],

          //column from which to extract the value

     to search for

          Sales[Country]

     ),

     BLANK()

)

027. Add a column from a table to another table if it satisfies more than one condition (2)
Table tools > new column

Tax by sale in Germany and Canada(6) =
//unrelated tables
//create a new column in table Sales
//the tax data is taken from the Country Tax table
//more than one condition must be met
IF(

     Country2[Country] IN {"Germany","Canada"},

     LOOKUPVALUE(

```
                //value to extract
                'Country Tax'[Tax],
                //search column
                'Country Tax'[Country],
                //column from which to extract the value
        to search for
                Sales[Country]
        ),
        BLANK()
)
```

028. Calculation of the accumulated by record
Table tools > new column

```
CashFlow by Reg=
//cash balance value per transaction
//expression, filter
CALCULATE (
        SUM ( CashFlow[Movement] ),
        FILTER (
                CashFlow,
                CashFlow[Reg] <= EARLIER (
        CashFlow[Reg] )
        )
)
```

029. Calculation of the accumulated per unit of time (1)
Table tools > new column

```
CashFlow by Date =
//cash balance value per transaction
//expression, filter
CALCULATE (
```

```
        SUM ( CashFlow[Movement] ),
        FILTER (
                CashFlow,
                CashFlow[Date] <= EARLIER (
        CashFlow[Date] )
        )
)
```

030. Calculation of the accumulated per unit of time (2)

Modeling > new measurement

```
Sales_2016 =
//calculation of an expression that is not affected by
context filters
//expression, filter
CALCULATE (
        SUM ( Sales[ Sales] ),
        FILTER (
                //ALL avoids the application of context
        filters outside the expression
                ALL ( Sales ),
                RELATED ( 'Calendar'[year] ) = 2016
        )
)
```

031. Calculation of the accumulated per unit of time (3)

Modeling > new measurement

```
Sales by Year =
//computation of an expression that is not affected by
context filters
//expression, filter
```

```
CALCULATE (
        SUM ( Sales[ Sales] ),
        FILTER (
                //ALL avoids the application of context
        filters outside the expression
                ALL ( Sales ),
                Sales[Date] <= MAX(Sales[Date])
        )
)
```

032. Count single values (1)
Modeling > new measurement

```
Number sales to Canada (1) =
//calculate the number of times a value is repeated
//expression, filter
CALCULATE (
        COUNT ( Sales[ Sales] ),
        //if affected by context filters
        Sales[Country] = "Canada"
)
```

033. Count single values (2)
Modeling > new measurement

```
Number sales to Canada (2) =
//calculate the number of times a value is repeated
//expression, filter
CALCULATE (
        COUNT ( Sales[ Sales] ),
        FILTER (
                //not affected by context filters
                ALL ( Sales ),
                Sales[Country] = "Canada"
        )
```

)

034. Count single values (3)
Modeling > new measurement

Number sales to Canada >5000(3) =
//Calculate the number of times that a value that meets
more than one condition is repeated
//expression, filter
CALCULATE(
        COUNT([Sales]),
        FILTER(
                //not affected by context filters
                ALL(Sales),
                AND(
                        Sales[Country]="Canada",
                        Sales[Sales]>5000
)
)
)

035. Count single values (4)
Modeling > new measurement

Number contries -sales (1) =
//count the number of unique values
//does affect context filters
DISTINCTCOUNT(Sales[Country])

036. Count single values (5)
Modeling > new measurement

Number contries -sales (2) =

18

//count the number of unique values
//do not affect context filters
CALCULATE(
        //count single values in text format
        DISTINCTCOUNTA(Sales[Country]),
        ALL(Sales)
)

037. Count single values (6)
Modeling > new measurement

Numbers of products sold (2) =
COUNTX(
        //we use FILTER to return a table
        FILTER(
                ALL(Sales),
                RELATED(Product [Product]) =
                Sales[Product]
        ),
        Sales[Sales]
)

038. Count single values (7)
Modeling > new measurement

Numbers of products sold (3) =
//expression, filter
CALCULATE(
        //count single values in text format - ignore blank
fields
        DISTINCTCOUNTNOBLANK(Sales[Product]),
        //specifies the direction of the filter to use
between two tables
        CROSSFILTER(
                'Product'[Product],

```
        Sales'[Product],
        Both
    )
)
```

039. Count single values (8)
Modeling > new measurement

```
Numbers of products sold (4) =
//expression, filter
CALCULATE(
        //count single values in text format - ignores blank
fields
        DISTINCTCOUNTNOBLANK(Sales[Product]),
        TREATAS(
                //filter table
                Country_3 ,
                //table on which the filter is applied
                'Country Tax'[Country]
        )
)
```

040. Count values for each category
Table tools > new table

```
Numbers of products sold (5) =
//counts the number of values using a second table as a
filter
//table from which data is extracted
SUMMARIZE(
        Sales,
        //data column
        Sales[Product],
        //column we create
        "numberSales", COUNTA(Sales[Product])
```

20

)

041. Count single values for each category
Table tools > new table

Numbers of products sold (6) =
//count the number of unique values using as filter a
second table
//table from which data is extracted
SUMMARIZE(
      Sales,
      //data column
      Sales[Product],
      //column we create between " " expression
      "numberSales", DISTINCTCOUNT(Sales[Product])
)

042. Count values of a category (1)
Modeling > new measurement

Number of sales to Germany (1) =
//count rows of a category. Context filters affect.
//expression, filter
CALCULATE(
      //expression: count rows
      COUNTROWS(Sales),
      //filter: by country Germany
      Sales[Country]="Germany"
)

043. Count values of a category (2)
Modeling > new measurement

```
Number of sales to Germany (2) =
//count rows of a category
//not affected by context filters
//expression, filter
CALCULATE(
        COUNTROWS(Sales),
        FILTER(
                //ALL avoids being affected by context
        filters.
                ALL(Sales),
                Sales[Country]="Germany"
        )
)
```

044. Count values of a category (3)

Modeling > new measurement

```
Number of sales to Germany (3) =
//count rows of a category ignoring rows with some blank
records
//not affected by context filters
//expression, filter
CALCULATE (
        //expression: count rows, ignoring rows with any
blank fields
        COUNTROWS ( Sales ),
        //filter: by country Germany
        FILTER (
                //table or expression returning a table
                ALLNOBLANKROW ( Sales ),
                //filtered field
                Sales[Country] = "Germany"
        )
)
```

22

045. Count filled fields
Modeling > new measurement

```
Number of NO blanks =
//count the number of values discarding blank fields
CALCULATE(
        //expression
        COUNT( Sales[Discounts]) ,
        //filter
        NOT( ISBLANK(Sales[Discounts]) )
)
```

046. Count empty fields
Modeling > new measurement

```
Number of blanks =
//count empty fields of a column
//affect context filters
COUNTBLANK(Sales[Discounts])
```

047. Count the number of times that each value of a category is repeated
Table tools > new column

```
Sales per Product (1) =
//Count the number of times each value is repeated
COUNTROWS(
        //table or expression returning a table
        FILTER(
                Sales,
                Sales[Product] = EARLIER(Sales[Product])
        )
)
```

048. Number of times that each value of a category that fulfills a condition is repeated.
Table tools > new column

Sales per Product (1) =
//Count the number of times each value is repeated
IF(
        //condition
        Sales[Product] = "Mouse" ,
        //positive result
        COUNTROWS(
                // table or expression returning a table
                FILTER(
                        Sales,
                        Sales[Product] =
                EARLIER(Sales[Product])
)
        ),
        //negative result
        BLANK()
)

049. Calculate Total (1)
Modeling > new measurement

Total sales (1) =
//if affected by context filters
SUM (Sales[Sales])

050. Calculate Total (2)
Modeling > new measurement

Total sales (2) =

24

```
//expression, filter
CALCULATE(
        SUM(Sales[ Sales]),
        //the ALL function avoids being affected by
context filters
        ALL(Sales)
)
```

051. Calculate Total by category (1)
Table tools > new table

```
Sales per Country and Sector =
//returns a table as result
//declare two variables
VAR gSales = SUM(Sales[ Sales])

VAR gTaxes = SUM(Sales[ Sales])*Sales[Tax]

RETURN

SUMMARIZE (
        //table from which we are going to calculate the
measure(s)
        Sales,
        //columns that are going to compose the table
        Sales[Country],
        Sales[Tax],
        Sales[Sector],
        //create the column(s) where the measures are
going to be calculated
        "grossSale", gSales,
        "netTax", gTaxes,
        "netSale", gSales – gTaxes
)
```

052. Calculate Total by category (2)
Table tools > new table

```
Sales per Sector in France =
//returns a table as result
CALCULATETABLE(
        //table or expression returning a table
        SUMMARIZE (
                //table from which we are going to
        calculate the measure(s)
                Sales,
                //columns that are going to compose the
        table
                Country Tax[Country],
                Sector[Sector],
                //create the column(s) where the
        measures are going to be calculated
                "totalSales", SUM ( Sales[ Sales] )
        ),
        //filters
        'Country Tax'[Country] = "France"
)
```

053. Calculate Total by category (3)
Table tools > new table

```
Sales per Midmarket Sector in France =
//returns a table as result
SUMMARIZE (
        //table or expression returning a table
        CALCULATETABLE(
                //table or expression returning a table
                Sales,
                //filters
                FILTER(
```

```
                Sector,
                Sector[Sector]="Midmarket"
                ),
                FILTER('Country Tax', 'Country
        Tax'[Country]="France"
                )
        ),
        //columns
        Category[Category],
        "totalSales", SUM ( Sales[ Sales] ),
        "Average Sales", AVERAGEX( Sales, SUM ( Sales[
Sales] ) ),
        "Max Sales", MAXX( Sales, SUM ( Sales[ Sales] ) ),
        "Min Sales", MINX( Sales, SUM ( Sales[ Sales] ) ),
        "Sales Count", COUNTROWS( Sales )
)
```

054. Calculate Subtotal by category (1)
Table tools > new table

```
Subtotal per Salesman and Sector (1) =
//columns are taken from several related tables
//at the beginning of the table shows the subtotal per
sector and seller
//at the end of the table the total per vendor
SUMMARIZECOLUMNS(
        ROLLUPADDISSUBTOTAL(
                Sales[Sector], "subtotal", Sales
        ),
        Salesman[Salesman],
        "Sales", SUM(Sales[ Sales])
)
```

27

055. Calculate Subtotal by category (2)
Table tools > new table

Subtotal per country (2) =
//columns are taken from one table only
//at the beginning of the table shows the subtotal per
sector and seller
//at the end of the table the total per vendor
SUMMARIZE(
        //table or expression returning a table
        Sales,
        Sales[Salesman],
        //group the result by sector
        ROLLUPGROUP(Sales[Sector]),
        "Sales", SUM(Sales[Sales])
)

056. Group result by N categories
Table tools > new table

Sales per salesman and country =
//works only in combination with other iterative
functions (SUMX,AVERAGEX,...)
GROUPBY (
        //table in which the calculations are performed
        Sales,
        //columns we are going to group by
        'Country Tax'[Country],
        Salesman[Salesman],
        //column(s) that will contain the calculation
        //GROUP BY always works with CURRENTGROUP
        "totalSales", SUMX (CURRENTGROUP (), SUM (
Sales[Sales]))
)

057. Compare two text strings same table

Table tools > new column

Compare two text strings (1) =
//compares two value strings
///is case-sensitive
EXACT(Sales[Gross Sales],Sales[Sales])

058. Compare two text strings different table

Table tools > new column

Compare two text strings (2) =
//compares two strings of values from two related tables
///is case-sensitive
EXACT(
       Country_2[Country] ,
       RELATED('Country Tax'[Country])
)

059. Mismatch values between two related tables

Table tools > new table

Countries without sales =
//returns a table with unique values
VAR countriesWithSales = VALUES(Sales[Country])

//returns a table with unique values
VAR countriesTable = VALUES(Country_2[Country])

//returns a table with the values that are in the first table
and not in the second table
//filtered table, filter table
VAR finalTable =

```
EXCEPT(
        countriesTable,
        countriesWithSales
)

RETURN

finalTable
```

060. Unmatched values between two unrelated tables
Table tools > new table

```
Countries without sales (2) =
//returns a table with unique values
VAR countriesWithSales = VALUES(Sales[Country])

//returns a table with unique values
VAR countriesTable = VALUES(Country_2[Country])

RETURN

//table, expression
CALCULATETABLE(
        //filtered table, filter table
        EXCEPT(
                countriesTable,
                countriesWithSales
        ),
        TREATAS(
                //filter table
                Country_3 ,
                //table on which the filter is applied
                'Country Tax'[Country]
        )
```

)

061. Matching values between two unrelated tables
Table tools > new table

Matching countries =
//matching values between two unrelated tables
//returns a table with no duplicate values
INTERSECT (
        VALUES (Country_3[Country]),
        VALUES (Country_2[Country])
)

062. Matching values between two related tables
Table tools > new column

Matching values =
//looks for matching values from the first table in the
second table
//related tables
EXACT(
        Country_2[Country] ,
        RELATED('Country Tax'[Country])
)

063. Rounding a figure up specifying number of decimal places
Table tools > new column

ROUND UP (2) =
//round a number away from zero
//table [column], decimal_number

ROUNDUP(Sales[Profit],2)

064. Rounding a figure down specifying number of decimal places
Table tools > new column

ROUND DOWN (2) =
//round a number towards zero
//table [column], decimal_number
ROUNDDOWN(Sales[Profit],2)

065. Rounding a digit to a number of decimals
Table tools > new column

ROUND =
//rounds a number to the specified number of decimal places
//table[column], decimal places
ROUND(Sales[Profit],2)

066. Rounding a figure down to its nearest significant multiple.
Table tools > new column

ROUND DOWN (1) =
//round a number to the nearest significant multiple downward
//table[column], multiply_value
FLOOR(Sales[Profit],0.10)

067. Rounding a digit up to its nearest significant multiple.

Table tools > new column

ROUND UP (1) =
//round a number to the nearest significant multiply upwards
//table[column], multiply_value
CEILING(Sales[Profit],0.10)

068. Rounding a digit down to the nearest whole number equal or lower

Table tools > new column

ROUND DOWN (1) =
//rounds a number to the nearest whole integer equal or lower
//table[column]
INT(Sales[Profit])

069. Return the integer part of a decimal number

Table tools > new column

ROUND (1) =
//returns the integer part of a number
//table[column]
TRUNC(Sales[Profit])

070. Add an exception to the results returned by a measure(1)

Modeling > new measurement

```
Total sales without USA =
//condition, is met shows result_1, is not met shows
result_2
IF (
        //HASONEVALUE discards empty fields inside
Sales[Country].
        HASONEVALUE ( Sales[Country] ),
        IF ( VALUES ( Sales[Country] ) <> "USA",
                SUM(Sales[ Sales]),
                BLANK ()
        ),
        CALCULATE(
                //expression, filter
                SUM(Sales[ Sales]),
                Sales[Country] <> "USA"
        )
)
```

071. Add an exception to the results returned by a measure(2)

Modeling > new measurement

```
Total sales USA and Germany =
//condition, is met shows result_1, is not met shows
result_2
IF (
        //HASONEVALUE discards empty fields inside
Sales[Country].
        HASONEVALUE ( Sales[Country] ),
        IF ( VALUES ( Sales[Country] ) IN {"USA",
        "Germany"},
                SUM(Sales[ Sales]),
                "Not included"
        ),
```

```
CALCULATE(
        //expression, filter
        SUM(Sales[ Sales]),
        Sales[Country] IN {"USA","Germany"}
    )
)
```

072. Calculation of an expression only if one or N specific conditions are selected.

Modeling > new measurement

```
Sales Germany 2016 =
//calculation of an expression only if one or more specific
conditions are selected
IF (
        //condition
        SELECTEDVALUE ( 'Calendar'[Year] ) = 2016 &&
        SELECTEDVALUE ( Sales[Country] ) = "Germany",
        //result if the condition is met
        SUM ( Sales[ Sales] ),
        //result if the condition is not met
        BLANK ()
)
```

073. Exclude from the calculation the rows containing any empty field

Table tools > new column

```
Net sale with discount =
//rows containing empty cells in the specified columns are
excluded from calculation
IF (
        //condition
```

```
AND (
          Sales[Gross Sales] <> BLANK() ,
          Sales[Discounts] <> BLANK()
     ),
     //result if the condition is met
     Sales[Gross Sales] - Sales[Discounts],
     //result if the condition is not fulfilled
     BLANK ()
)
```

074. Show all values even if they are zeros

Table tools > new column

```
Discounts (1) =
//in a chart show all values even if they are zeros
//in a table replace blank values in a column with zeros
Sales[Discounts] + 0
```

075. Maximum value of a total

Modeling > new measurement

```
Total best selling product (5) =
//calculate the total of the best-selling product
//create a variable that obtains a summary table by total
product sales
VAR baseTable =
     SUMMARIZE(
          //table or expression returning a table
          Sales,
          //column
          Sales[Product],
          //expression
          "totalSale",SUM(Sales[ Sales])
     )
```

RETURN

MAXX(
        //table
        baseTable,
        //expression
        [totalSale]
)

076. Field name of the maximum value of a total

STEP.1
Continuing with the previous example, let's find out the name of the best selling product. To do this, we must first perform point 075.

STEP.2
Table tools > new table

Summary table =
SUMMARIZE(
                Sales,
                Sales[Product],
                "totalSale", SUM(Sales[Sales])
)

STEP.3
Modeling > new measurement

Top selling product name =
//result_column, search_column, expression,
result_if_it_is_not_found
LOOKUPVALUE(
                'Summary table'[Product],

37

```
        'Summary table'[totalSale],
        [Total best selling product (5)],
        "There is more than one value"
        )
```

077. Create a measure by filtering the result from N related tables (1)

Modeling > new measurement

```
Sales France 2016 (1) =
// create a measure (iterator) filtering the result from
several related tables
SUMX(
        //table or expression returning a table
        FILTER(
                Sales,
                AND(
                        RELATED ( 'Country Tax'[Country] )
                = "France",
                        RELATED ( 'Calendar'[year] ) =
                2016
                )
        ),
        //expression
        Sales[ Sales]
)
```

078. Create a measure by filtering the result from N related tables (2)

Modeling > new measurement

```
Sales France 2016 (2) =
//create a measure (non-iterator) by filtering the result
from several related tables
```

```
CALCULATE (
        //expression
        SUM ( Sales[ Sales] ),
        //filter
        FILTER (
                Sales,
                AND (
                        RELATED ( 'Country Tax'[Country] )
                = "France",
                        RELATED ( 'Calendar'[year] ) =
                2016
                )
        )
)
```

079. Get a sample N of a specific field
Table tools > new table

```
Sales sample  =
//get a random sample of the values in a row
//sample_size, table, column, order
SAMPLE ( 10, Sales, Sales[Sales ID], ASC )
```

080. Obtain a sample N from a specific field satisfying N conditions
Table tools > new table

```
Sales sample Germany 2016 =
//get a random sample of the values in a column that
satisfy one or more of the following conditions
CALCULATETABLE(
        //table or expression returning a table
        //sample_size, table, column, order
        SAMPLE(10, Sales, Sales[Sales ID], ASC),
```

```
        //filter
        FILTER(
                Sales,
                AND(
                        Sales[Country]="Germany",
                        RELATED('Calendar'[year])=2016
                )
        )
)
```

081. Create a column or measure that satisfies a
condition with respect to another column (1)
Table tools > new column

```
Sales type (2) -BOOLE =
//create a column that satisfies a condition with respect
to another column
IF(
        //condition
        Sales[ Sales]<15000,
        //result if the condition is met
        //table[column], expression, result, expression,
result..., remainder
        SWITCH(
                TRUE(),
                Sales[Country]="Canada","LOW",
                Sales[Country]="Germany","NORMAL",
                Sales[Country]="France","LOW",
                Sales[Country]="UK","LOW",
                Sales[Country]="USA","LOW",
                Sales[Country]="Mexico","NORMAL",
                "Unknow"
        ),
        //result if the condition is not met
        IF(
                //condition
```

```
        AND(Sales[ Sales]>15001,Sales[
Sales]<30000),
        //result if the condition is met
        //table[column], expression, result,
expression, result..., remainder
        SWITCH(
                TRUE(),
                Sales[Country]="Canada",
                "NORMAL",
                Sales[Country]="Germany",
                "HIGH",
                Sales[Country]="France",
                "NORMAL",
                Sales[Country]="UK",
                "HIGH",
                Sales[Country]="USA",
                "NORMAL",
                Sales[Country]="Mexico",
                "HIGH",
                "Unknow"
        ),
        //result if the condition is not met
        IF(
                //condition
                Sales[ Sales]>3001,
                //result if the condition is met
                //table[column], expression,
        result, expression, result..., remainder
                SWITCH(
                        TRUE(),
                        Sales[Country]="Canada",
                        "HIGH",
                        Sales[Country]=
                        "Germany","HIGH",
                        Sales[Country]="France",
                        "HIGH",
                        Sales[Country]="UK",
```

```
                                    "HIGH",
                                    Sales[Country]="USA",
                                    "HIGH",
                                    Sales[Country]="Mexico",
                                    "HIGH",
                                    "Unknow"
                         ) ,
                         //result if the condition is not met
                         BLANK()
             )
         )
)
```

082. Create a column or measure that satisfies a condition with respect to another column (2)

Table tools > new column

```
Continent (1) =
//create a column that satisfies a condition with respect
to another column
SWITCH(
        TRUE(),
        Sales[Country]="Canada","AMERICA",
        Sales[Country]="Germany","EUROPE",
        Sales[Country]="France","EUROPE",
        Sales[Country]="UK","EUROPE",
        Sales[Country]="USA","AMERICA",
        "Unknow"
)
```

083. Create a column or measure that satisfies a condition with respect to another column (3)

Table tools > new column

```
Continent (2) =
//create a column that satisfies a condition with respect
to another column
SWITCH(
        Sales[Country],
        "Canada","AMERICA",
        "Germany","EUROPE",
        "France","EUROPE",
        "UK","EUROPE",
        "USA","AMERICA",
        "Unknow"
)
```

084. Create a table that filters the values for a slicer
Table tools > new table

```
Filtered by country =
//get filtering values for a slicer
FILTERS(Sales[Country])
```

085. Rank N concepts (1)
Table tools > new table

```
Top 2 products sales (1) =
//name of the 2 best selling products
//create a variable that returns a table
VAR salesPerProduct =
        SUMMARIZE (
                Sales,
                Sales[Product],
                "totalSales", SUM ( Sales[ Sales] )
                )
RETURN

TOPN ( 2, salesPerProduct, [totalSales] )
```
43

086. Rank N concepts (2)
Modeling > new measurement

Top 2 products sales (2) =
//total value of the sales of the 2 best-selling products
//we set for the calculation of the table obtained in point 085
SUM('Top 2 products sales (1)'[totalSales])

087. Rank N concepts (3)
Table tools > new table

```
Top 2 products sales in Canada =
VAR salesPerProduct =
CALCULATETABLE(
        //table
        SUMMARIZE (
                Sales,
                'Calendar'[year],
                Sales[Country],
                Sales[Product],
                "totalSales", SUM ( Sales[ Sales] )
        ),
        //filter
        Sales[Country] = "Canada"
)

RETURN

TOPN ( 2, salesPerProduct, [totalSales] )
```


088. Rank N concepts (4)
Modeling > new measurement

Salesman ranking (1) =
//returns the position within the range of each resulting
value
IF(
        HASONEVALUE(Sales[Salesman]),
        //result if the condition is met
        RANKX(ALL(Sales[Salesman]),[Total Sales],,DESC),
        //result if the condition is not met
        BLANK()
)

089. Rank N concepts (5)
Modeling > new measurement

Salesman ranking (2) =
//shows the ranking of sellers for the selected year
//regardless of the other context filters
CALCULATE(
        //expression
        IF(
                //condition
                HASONEVALUE(Sales[Salesman]),
                //result if the condition is met
                RANKX(
                        ALL(Sales[Salesman]),
                        [Total Sales],,DESC
                ),
                //result if the condition is not fulfilled
                BLANK()
                ),
        //filter
        ALLSELECTED('Calendar'[year])
)

090. Rank N concepts (6)

Modeling > new measurement

```
Salesman ranking (3) =
IF(
        //condition
        ISINSCOPE(Sales[Product]),
        //result if the condition is met
        RANKX(
                //ALL avoids the application of context
        filters outside the expression
                ALL(Sales[Product]),
                [Total Sales]
        ),
        //result if the condition is not met
        IF(
                //condition
                ISINSCOPE(Sales[Category]),
                //result if the condition is met
                RANKX(
                        //ALL avoids the application of
                context filters outside the expression
                        ALL(Sales[Category]),
                        [Total Sales]

                )

        )

)
```

091. Inverse ranking N concepts

Modeling > new measurement

```
Bottom Ranked Products =
//ranking of the three products with less sales
VAR SalesTable =
FILTER(
        VALUES('Product'[Product]),
```

```
        [Total Sales] > 0
)

RETURN

CONCATENATEX(
        TOPN(
                3,
                SalesTable,
                [Total Sales],
                ASC
        ),
        'Product'[Product],
        ", "
)
```

092. Forcing a second relationship between tables
Modeling > new measurement

```
Sales per date2 (1) =
//force a second relationship between tables
//go in Power BI to relationships and drag with the mouse
the field "Calendar[Date]" over the field "Sales[Date2]".
//now we create the action
CALCULATE (
        //expression
        SUM ( Sales[ Sales] ),
        //filter
        //relationship_type_table_to_several,
relationship_type_table_to_one
        USERELATIONSHIP ( Sales[Date2], Calendar[Date] )
)
```

093. Fill blanks in a column with zeros (1)
Modeling > new measurement

Discount Blank (1) =
//fill blank fields of a column with zeros
//returns the first expression that does not evaluate to
BLANK
COALESCE(
        SELECTEDVALUE(Sales[Discounts]),
        0
)

094. Fill blanks in a column with zeros (2)
Modeling > new measurement

Discount Blank (2) =
//prevents the result of an expression from being a blank
field
//returns the first expression that does not evaluate to
BLANK
//condition, positive result, negative result
IF(
        //condition
        ISBLANK(SELECTEDVALUE(Sales[Discounts])),
        //result if the condition is met
        0,
        //result if the condition is not met
        SELECTEDVALUE(Sales[Discounts])
)

095. Create a column or measure that is not affected by context filters
Modeling > new measurement

Netop V10 sales =

```
//calculate a result for a column without being affected by
any context filters
//expression, filter
CALCULATE (
        SUM ( Sales[ Sales] ),
        //the ALL function avoids the application of any
context filters
        ALL ( Sales )
)
```

096. Create a column or measure with N filtered conditions from the same table

Modeling > new measurement

```
Total sales Germany/Tower (1) =
//application of the ALL command to several tables on
which we are going to apply a condition
//expression, filter
CALCULATE(
        SUM(Sales[ Sales]),
        FILTER(
                //ALL avoids the application of context
        filters outside the expression
                ALL(Sales),
                AND(
                        Sales[Country] = "Germany",
                        Sales[Product] = "Tower"
                )
        )
)
```

097. Create a column or measure with N conditions filtered from several tables

Modeling > new measurement

Total sales Germany/Tower (2) =
//application of the ALL command to several tables on
which we are going to apply a condition
//expression, filter
CALCULATE(
    SUM(Sales[Sales]),
    FILTER(
        //ALL avoids the application of context
    filters outside the expression
        ALL(Sales),
        AND(
            RELATED('Country Tax'[Country]) =
            "Germany",
            RELATED(Product[Product]) =
            "Tower"
)
)
)

098. Create a column or measure where a context
filter affects a specific field only
Modeling > new measurement

Total sales per selected month =
//the filter only affects one field
//create a variable
VAR totalSales =
SUM(Sales[Sales])

RETURN

CALCULATE(
    totalSales,

//ALLSELECTED removes context filters from columns and rows of the query being performed except on the table [column] it contains
     ALLSELECTED(Calendar[Month])
)

099. Create a column or measure where "N" context filters affect only "N" specific fields
Modeling > new measurement

Percent of total per country and product =
//filters that affect more than one field
VAR totalSales =
SUM(Sales[Sales])

RETURN

CALCULATE(
     //expression
     totalSales,
     //filter
     ALLSELECTED(Product[Product]),
     ALLSELECTED('Country Tax'[Country])
)

100. Create a column or measure filtered from N tables
Modeling > new measurement

Sales Hardware (1) =
//result is obtained that meets the conditions of a filter that belongs to the same table and a second filter that belongs to a second table.
CALCULATE(

```
//expression
SUM(Sales[ Sales]),
//filter
FILTER(
        //table
        Sales,
        //filter
        AND(
                Sales[Units Sold] > 1000 ,
                //filter through a column of a
        related table
                RELATED(Category[Category])=
                "Hardware"
        )
    )
)
```

101. Calculate cumulative measure (1)
Modeling > new measurement

```
Cumulative Sales (1) =
//calculate a cumulative measure
//expression, filter
CALCULATE(
        //expression
        SUM ( Sales[ Sales] ),
        //filter
        FILTER (
                //the ALL function prevents it from being
        affected by context filters
                ALL ( Sales ),
                Sales[Date] <= MAX ( Sales[Date])
        )
)
```

102. Calculate cumulative measure (2)

Modeling > new measurement

```
Cumulative Sales (2) =
//calculate a cumulative measure
//expression, filter
CALCULATE(
        //expression
        SUM(Sales[ Sales]),
        //only affected by the context filter `Year`.
        FILTER(
                ALLEXCEPT(Sales, 'Calendar'[year]),
                Sales[Date]<=MAX(Sales[Date])
        )
)
```

103. Calculate number of unique rows

Table tools > new column

STEP 1
```
Text String =
//create column that combines values from several
columns
//delimiter, table1[column1], table1[column2],...,
table1[columnN]
COMBINEVALUES(
        " ",
            Sales[Country],
            Sales[Category],
            Sales[Product]
            )
```

STEP 2
Modeling > new measurement

Unique values per row =
DISTINCTCOUNT(Sales[Text String])

104. Table rows with unique values
Table tools > new table

Single rows =
VALUES(Sales[Text String])

105. Calculate number of repeated values in a column
Modeling > new measurement

Repeated countries =
//count the number of times the countries are repeated
COUNT(Sales[Country]) - DISTINCTCOUNT(Sales[Country])

106. Calculate number of times a specific value is repeated in a column
Modeling > new measurement

Repeated countries (Canada) =
//count the number of times "Canada" is repeated
CALCULATE(
        //expression
        COUNT(Sales[Country]) - DISTINCTCOUNT(
Sales[Country]),
        //filter
        Sales[Country]="Canada"
)

107. Number of times a condition (x) is fulfilled (1)
Modeling > new measurement

Number of sales of a product -MOUSE (1) =
//count the number of times a value appears in text
//not affected by context filters
CALCULATE(
        //expression
        COUNTAX (
                //table
                //ALL avoids the application of context
        filters outside the expression
                ALL (Sales),
                //expression
                Sales[Product]
        ),
        //filter
        Sales[Product]="Mouse"
)

108. Number of times a condition (x) is fulfilled (2)

Modeling > new measurement

Number of sales of a product -MOUSE (1) =
//count the number of times a value appears in text
//if you are affected by context filters
CALCULATE(
        //expression
        COUNTAX (
                //table
                Sales,
                //expression
                Sales[Product]
        ),
        //filter
        Sales[Product]="Mouse"
)

109. Number of times a condition (x) is fulfilled (3)
Modeling > new measurement

Number of sales <10k =
//count the number of times a numerical value is displayed
//if you are affected by context filters

```
CALCULATE(
        //expression
        COUNTX(
                //table
                Sales,
                //expression
                Sales[ Sales]
        ),
        //filter
        FILTER(Sales, Sales[ Sales]<10000)
)
```

110. Number of times a condition (x) is fulfilled (4)
Modeling > new measurement

Number of sales <10k (2) =
//count the number of times a numerical value is displayed
//not affected by context filters
```
CALCULATE(
        //expression
        COUNTX(
                //table
                ALL(Sales),
                //expression
                Sales[ Sales]
        ),
        //filter
```

        FILTER(Sales, Sales[Sales]<10000)
)

111. Find a row containing specified values
Modeling > new measurement

Row containing the values =
//search for a row in the "Localization" table that contains the specified values
//measurement yields TRUE or FALSE results
//table, column_1, column_2, column_3...
CONTAINSROW(Localization,"Germany","Berlin")

112. Find a column containing specified values
Modeling > new measurement

Sales to Italy =
//measurement yields TRUE or FALSE results
CONTAINS(Sales, Sales[Country],"Italy")

113. Condition: LESS THAN

Calculated_Column =
IF(
        //condition
        Sales[Sales]<10000,
        //result if the condition is met
        TRUE(),
        //result if the condition is not fulfilled
        FALSE()
)

114. Condition: GREATER THAN

```
Calculated_Column =
IF(
        //condition
        Sales[ Sales]>10000,
        //result if the condition is met
        TRUE(),
        //result if the condition is not fulfilled
        FALSE()
)
```

115. Condition: OTHER THAN

```
Calculated_Column =
IF(
        //condition
        Sales[Product]<>"Netop V10",
        //result if the condition is met
        TRUE(),
        //result if the condition is not fulfilled
        FALSE()
)
```

116. Condition: AND (1)

```
Calculated_Column =
IF(
        //condition
        Sales[Country]="Canada"  &&
        Sales[Sector]="Midmarket" ,
        //result if the condition is met
        TRUE(),
        //result if the condition is not fulfilled
```

```
        FALSE()
)
```

```
Calculated_Column =
IF(
        //condition
        AND(
                Sales[Country]="Canada" ,
                Sales[Sector]="Midmarket"
        ),
        //result if the condition is met
        TRUE(),
        //result if the condition is not fulfilled
        FALSE()
)
```

```
Calculated_Column =
IF(
        //condition
        Sales[Country]="Canada" ||
         Sales[Sector]="Midmarket",
        //result if the condition is met
        TRUE(),
        //result if the condition is not fulfilled
        FALSE()
)
```

119. Condition: OR (2)

```
Calculated_Column =
IF(
        //condition
        OR(Sales[Country]="Canada",
        Sales[Sector]="Midmarket"),
        //result if the condition is met
        TRUE(),
        //result if the condition is not fulfilled
        FALSE()
)
```

120. Condition: LESS THAN OR EQUAL TO

```
Calculated_Column =
IF(
        //condition
        Sales[ Sales]<=10000,
        //result if the condition is met
        TRUE(),
        //result if the condition is not fulfilled
        FALSE()
)
```

121. Condition: GREATER THAN OR EQUAL TO

```
Calculated_Column =
IF(
        //condition
        Sales[ Sales]>=10000,
        //result if the condition is met
        TRUE(),
```

```
//result if the condition is not fulfilled
        FALSE()
)
```

122. Condition: BETWEEN

```
Number of sales between 100 and 1000 units =
//expression: between two values (quantities, dates,..)
CALCULATE (
        //expression
        COUNTROWS(Sales),
        //filter
        FILTER (
                //table
                Sales,
                //filter
                AND(
                        Sales[Units Sold] > 100 ,
                        Sales[Units Sold] < 1000

                )
        )
)
```

123. Condition: INCLUDED

```
Product sold (1) =
CALCULATE (
        //expression
        SUM ( Sales[ Sales] ),
        //filter
        //the expression is calculated for each row
containing one of the three products
        FILTER(
                //table
                Sales,
```

```
            //filter
            Sales[Product] IN { "Mouse", "Keyboard",
      "Paper" }
            )
)
```

124. Condition: NOT INCLUDED

```
Product sold (2) =
CALCULATE (
        //expression
        SUM ( Sales[ Sales] ),
        //filter
        //expression is calculated for each row that does
NOT contain any of the three products
        FILTER(
                //table
                Sales,
                //filter
                NOT(Sales[Product]) IN { "Mouse",
                "Keyboard", "Paper" }

        )
)
```

125. Condition: NO

```
Sales target =
//returns TRUE or FALSE
NOT ( Sales[ Sales] < 10000 )
```

126. Condition: YES
Table tools > new column

Discounts (2) =
IF (
        //condition: empty field of table [column]
specified
        Sales[Discounts]>1000 ,
        //positive result specified by us
        "HIGH",
        //negative result specified by us
        "LOW"
)

127. Condition: IF.ERROR

Applied discount =
//in case the precondition is NOT met the resultant value
is defined by us
IFERROR(
        //expression
        DIVIDE(Sales[COGS], Sales[Discounts]),
        //result defined by us in case the error expression
is not met
        BLANK()
)

128. Condition: BLANK IF FIELD
Table tools > new column

Discounts (1) =
//if a field is blank the positive result applies

```
//if a field is NOT blank apply the negative result
IF(
        //condition: empty field of table [column]
specified
        ISBLANK(Sales[Discounts]),
        //positive result specified by us
        "not applied",
        //negative result specified by us
        "applied"
)
```

129. Condition: FIELD NOT BLANK
Table tools > new column

```
Discounts (1) =
//if a field is blank, the positive result applies
//if a field is NOT blank apply the negative result
IF(
        //condition: empty field of table [column]
specified
        NOT( ISBLANK(Sales[Discounts])),
        //positive result specified by us
        "not applied",
        //negative result specified by us
        "applied"
)
```

130. First value that fulfills a condition (1)
Modeling > new measurement

```
Total discounts per salesman =
FIRSTNONBLANKVALUE(
        //column
        Sales[Salesman],
        //expression
```

```
      SUM(Sales[Discounts])
)
```

131. First value that fulfills a condition (2)
Modeling > new measurement

```
First sale =
FIRSTNONBLANK (
      //column
      Sales[Salesman],
      //expression
      CALCULATE(SUM(Sales[Discounts]))
)
```

132. Last value meeting condition (1)
Modeling > new measurement

```
Last sale =
LASTNONBLANK (
      //column
      Sales[Salesman],
      //expression
      CALCULATE(SUM(Sales[Discounts]))
)
```

133. Last value meeting condition (2)
Modeling > new measurement

```
Total discounts per salesman =
LASTNONBLANKVALUE(
      //column
      Sales[Salesman],
      //expression
```

```
        SUM(Sales[Discounts])
)
```

134. First value satisfying more than one condition (1)

Modeling > new measurement

```
First purchase amount per customer -Canada 2016  =
CALCULATE (
        //expression
        FIRSTNONBLANKVALUE (
                //column
                Sales[Sector],
                //expression
                SUM ( Sales[ Sales] )
        ),
        //filter
        FILTER (
                //table
                //the ALL function prevents it from being
        affected by context filters
                ALL ( Sales ),
                //filter
                AND (
                        Sales[Country] = "Canada",
                        //filter through a column of a
                related table
                        RELATED('Calendar'[year]) = 2016
                )
        )
)
```

135. First value satisfying more than one condition (2)

Modeling > new measurement

```
First purchase amount per customer in Midmarket Sector
-Canada 2016  =
CALCULATE (
        //expression
        FIRSTNONBLANKVALUE (
                //column
                Sales[Sector],
                //expression
                SUM ( Sales[ Sales] )
        ),
        //filter
        FILTER (
                //do not affect context filters
                //table
                ALL ( Sales ),
                //filter
                AND (
                        Sales[Country] = "Canada",
                        //filter through a column of a
                related table
                        RELATED ( 'Calendar'[year] ) =
                2016
                        )
        ),
        FILTER (
                //table
                Sector,
                //filter
                Sector[Sector] = "Midmarket"
        )
)
```

136. Last value that meets more than one condition (1)

Modeling > new measurement

Last purchase amount per customer -Canada 2016 =
CALCULATE (
        //expression
        LASTNONBLANKVALUE (
                //column
                Sales[Sector],
                //expression
                SUM (Sales[Sales])
        ),
        FILTER (
                //do not affect context filters
                //table
                ALL (Sales),
                //expression
                AND (
                        Sales[Country] = "Canada",
                        //filter through a column of a
                related table
                        RELATED('Calendar'[year]) = 2016
)
)
)

137. Last value that meets more than one condition (2)

Modeling > new measurement

Last purchase amount per customer in Midmarket Sector -
Canada 2016 =
CALCULATE (
        //expression

```
LASTNONBLANKVALUE (
        //column
        Sales[Sector],
        //expression
        SUM ( Sales[ Sales] )
),
FILTER (
        //do not affect context filters
        //table
        ALL ( Sales ),
        //filter
        AND (
                Sales[Country] = "Canada",
                //filter through a column of a
        related table
                RELATED ( 'Calendar'[year] ) =
        2016
                )
),
FILTER (
        //table
        Sector,
        //filter
        Sector[Sector] = "Midmarket"
        )
)
)
```

138. Calculating a measure ignoring empty fields
Modeling > new measurement

```
Salesmans total sales =
//discards sales where the "Discounts" field is empty
CALCULATE(
        //expression
        SUM( Sales [Sales]),
        //filter
```

```
FILTER(
        //table
        Sales,
        //filter
        NOT (ISBLANK(Sales[Discounts]))
    )
)
```

139. Calculate a measure ignoring fields that contain a specific value
Modeling > new measurement

```
Total Sales -not Canada =
//the measure discards in the calculation the values
corresponding to Canada
CALCULATE(
        //expression
        SUM( Sales [Sales]),
        //filter
        FILTER(
                //table
                Sales,
                //filter
                Sales[Country] <> "Canada"
        )
)
```

140. Substitute one value for another
Table tools > new column

```
Continent =
//substitute one value for another in a new column
SWITCH (
        TRUE (),
```

'Country Tax'[Country] = "Canada", "American",
'Country Tax'[Country] = "Germany", "European",
'Country Tax'[Country] = "France", "European",
'Country Tax'[Country] = "Mexico", "American",
'Country Tax'[Country] = "USA", "American",
'Country Tax'[Country] = "UK", "European",
//and if it is none of the above leave the field
blank
BLANK ()
)

141. Find a specific text within a text string (1)
Table tools > new column

FIND "John" =
//looks for the position (counting from the left) of the first
occurrence of a character or of a text string inside another
text string
// DOES discriminate between upper and lower case
letters
IFERROR(
FIND("John", Salesman[Salesman]),BLANK()
)

142. Find a specific text within a text string (2)
Table tools > new column

SEARCH "John" =
//looks for the position (counting from the left) of the first
occurrence of a character or of a text string inside another
text string
///NOT case-sensitive
IFERROR(
SEARCH("John",Salesman[Salesman]), BLANK()
)

143. Make text lowercase
Table tools > new column

Lowercase text =
//shift text to lowercase
LOWER(Salesman[Salesman])

144. Make text uppercase
Table tools > new column

Uppercase text =
//upset text to uppercase
UPPER(Salesman[Salesman])

145. Extract text from a text string
Table tools > new column

Extract text =
//extract a text string
//text, initial_position, number_characters
MID(Salesman[Salesman], 3, 2)

146. Find text within a text string and extract it
Table tools > new column

Search and Extract =
//search and extract a text within a text string
IFERROR(
        //expression to be fulfilled
        MID(
                Salesman[Salesman],
                SEARCH("John", Salesman[Salesman]),
                2

72

),
//result in case of non-compliance
BLANK()
)

147. Replace one value in a text string with another value in a text string
Table tools > new column

Replace text string (1) =
//delete a 2 character string starting at position 3
//and replaces it with a single character
REPLACE(Salesman[Salesman], 3, 2, "_")

148. Find and replace a value in a text string with another value
Table tools > new column

Replace text string (2) =
//searches and removes a string and replaces it with a text
string
IFERROR(
        //expression to be fulfilled
        REPLACE(
                Salesman[Salesman],
                SEARCH("h",Salesman[Salesman]), 2, "_"
        ),
        //result in case of non-compliance
        BLANK()
)

149. Insert a value into a text string
Table tools > new column

Insert text string (1) =
//inserts a text string at the specified position without deleting anything
//for this we use the value 0
REPLACE(Salesman[Salesman], 3, 0, "_")

150. Insert a value at the beginning of a text string.
Table tools > new column

InsertInsert text string (2) =
//inserts a text string at the beginning without deleting anything
REPLACE(Salesman[Salesman], 1, 0, "_")

151. Insert a value at the end of a text string
Table tools > new column

Insert text string (3) =
//inserts a text string at the end without deleting anything
//the 100 represents a field length not exceeded by the contents of the fields in the column
REPLACE(Salesman[Salesman], 100, 1, "_")

152. Extract text from a text string (1)
Table tools > new column

Extract text from right =
//extract a number of characters from right to left
//table[column];number_of_characters

RIGHT(Salesman[Salesman],4)

153. Extract text from a text string (2)
Table tools > new column

Extract text from left =
//extract a number of characters from left to right
//table[column];number_of_characters
LEFT(Salesman[Salesman],4)

154. Replacing one or N characters with other characters
Table tools > new column

Replace blanks =
//replace blank spaces with "_".
//table[Column]; old_text; new_text
SUBSTITUTE(Salesman[Salesman]," ","_")

155. Removes whitespace from text and inserts a single space between each word
Table tools > new column

Remove blanks =
//replace blanks in the text with a single blank space
between each word
TRIM(Salesman[Salesman])

156. Text search. Case insensitive (1)
Table tools > new column

Search "owe" =

///NOT case-sensitive
//the "?" symbol represents any character, e.g. "Tower"
would fit the query
//table[column],text_to_search
CONTAINSSTRING(Product[Product],"?owe?")

157. Text search. Case insensitive (2)
Table tools > new column

Search "owe" =
///NOT case-sensitive
//the symbol "*" represents any set of characters, e.g.
"Tower" and "Power BI" would fit in the query
//table[column], text_to_search
CONTAINSSTRING(Product[Product],"*owe*")

158. Text search. Case sensitive.
Table tools > new column

Search "Power" =
//DOES discriminate between upper and lower case
letters
//table[column],text_to_search
CONTAINSSTRINGEXACT(Product[Product],"Power")

159. Concatenate columns (1)
Table tools > new column

Join Localization and Province (1) =
//join values from different columns
CONCATENATE(Localization[Country],
Localization[Province])

160. Concatenate columns (2)

Table tools > new column

Join Localization and Province (2) =
//we use "&" for joining two or more columns with a separator
//separator is specified in quotation marks
Localization[Country]&","&Localization[Province]

161. Concatenate columns (3)

Table tools > new column

Join country, category and product =
//concatenate more than two fields per row using a separator
COMBINEVALUES(
        //delimiter
        ",",
        // table1[column1]
        Sales[Country],
        // table1[column2],..,
        Sales[Category],
        // table1[columnN]
        Sales[Product]
)

162. Display an expression on a card that results in more than one value

Modeling > new measurement

Ranked Products -view on card =
//declare one variable
VAR salesPerProduct =
SUMMARIZE (

```
        //table or expression returning a table
        Sales,
        //column
        Sales[Product],
        //calculated column
        "totalSales", SUM ( Sales[ Sales] )
)

RETURN

//the function , is only an example, you can substitute it
for any other one
CONCATENATEX(
        //table or expression returning a table
        TOPN (
                3,
                salesPerProduct,
                [totalSales]
        ),
        Sales[Product],
        ", "
)
```

163. Calculate a % from totals (1)

Table tools > new column

```
Gross profit (1) =
//returns as result an integer number
//results NULL are replaced by 0
QUOTIENT(Sales[ Sales],Sales[COGS])
```

164. Calculate a % from totals (2)

Table tools > new column

```
Gross profit (2) =
```

//percentage of gross margin on sales
//result in a decimal number
//results NULL are replaced by 0
DIVIDE(Sales[COGS],Sales[Sales])

165. Calculate a % from totals (3)
Modeling > new measurement

Gross profit (3) =
//returns as result an integer number
//results NULL are replaced by 0
VAR totalSales = SUM(Sales[Sales])

VAR totalCOGS = SUM(Sales[COGS])

RETURN

DIVIDE(totalCOGS,totalSales)

166. Calculate a % from totals (4)
Table tools > new column

Gross profit (4) =
//specifies number of decimal places equal to 2
//percentage of gross margin on sales
//result in a decimal number
//results NULL are replaced by 0
ROUND(DIVIDE(Sales[COGS],Sales[Sales]),2)

167. Calculate maximum value per category
Modeling > new measurement

Last ID sale per Category =

```
//last sales record by category
MAXX(
        //table
        Sales,
        //expression
        Sales[Sales ID]
)
```

168. Calculate minimum value per category

Modeling > new measurement

```
First ID sale per Category =
//first sales record by category
MINX(
        //filtered value
        Sales,
        //expression
        Sales[Sales ID]
)
```

169. Select measure from a list

STEP 1: Modeling > new measurement
```
//create N measures separately, in this case two
AverageS = AVERAGE(Sales[ Sales])
TotalS = SUM(Sales[ Sales])
```

STEP 2: home > data entry
```
//create a new table and call it "Measure" and its column
"Calculation".
//in the column "Calculation" we add two records
"averageSale" and "totalSale".
//this table is used in a "slicer"
```

STEP 3: Modeling > new measurement
//this measure can be used in a "graph, matrix, table".
//it will represent the option that is selected in the slicer
Calculation type =
SWITCH(
        SELECTEDVALUE(Measure[Calculation]),
        //column name, expression
        "averageSale", [AverageS],
        //column name, expression
        "totalSale", [TotalS],
        // remainder
        ""
)

170. Value of a field between two dates
Modeling > new measurement

Sales from 01/05/2013 to 30/05/2014 =
//value of a field within a date range
CALCULATE(
        //expression
        SUM(Sales[Sales]),
        //filter
        DATESBETWEEN(
                //table
                Calendar[Date],
                //start date
                DATE(2013,05,01),
                //end date
                DATE(2014,05,30)
)
)

171. Calculate value of a measure from a date up to N time units (1)

Modeling > new measurement

```
SalesSales last 15 days =
CALCULATE(
        //expression
        SUM(Sales[ Sales]),
        //filter
        DATESINPERIOD(
                //table
                'Calendar'[Date],
                //origin date
                TODAY(),
                //period
                -14,DAY
        )
)
```

172. Calculate value of a measure from a date up to N time units (2)

Table tools > new column

```
Sales last 40 days =
//expression, filter
CALCULATE(
    SUM(Sales[ Sales]),
    FILTER(
        //table
        ALL('Calendar'),
        //filter
        Calendar[Date]>=TODAY()-40 &&
        Calendar[Date]<TODAY()
    )
)
```

173. Calculate value of a measure from a date up to N time units

Modeling > new measurement

```
Current month sales =
//executes an expression from the first day of the
CURRENT month until now
//measurement is reset to zero at the beginning of each
month
TOTALMTD(
        //expression
        SUM(Sales[ Sales]),
        //table
        'Calendar'[Date]
)
```

174. Calculate the value of a measure from the beginning of the quarter to the last date of the current context

Modeling > new measurement

```
Current quarter sales =
//runs an expression from the first day of the CURRENT
quarter until now
//measurement is reset to zero at the beginning of each
quarter
TOTALQTD(
        //expression
        SUM(Sales[ Sales]),
        //table
        'Calendar'[Date]
)
```

175. Calculate the value of a measure from the beginning of the year to the last date of the current context

Modeling > new measurement

Current year sales (1)=
//executes an expression from the first day of the current year until now
//measurement is reset to zero at the beginning of each year
TOTALYTD(
       //expression
       SUM(Sales[Sales]),
       //table
       'Calendar'[Date]
)

176. Calculate the value of a measure on the current day.

Modeling > new measurement

Sales today =
//calculation of an expression with current day value
CALCULATE(
       //expression
       SUM(Sales[Sales]),
       //filter
       Sales[Date] = TODAY()
)

177. Calculate the time difference between two dates

Modeling > new measurement

Days per sent =
//difference of time between two dates
DATEDIFF(Sales[Date2],Sales[Date],DAY)

178. Average
Modeling > new measurement

Average sales =
//average sales amount
AVERAGE(Sales[Sales])

179. Conditional sum
Modeling > new measurement

Sales on Germany =
//sum values if they meet a condition
SUMX(
        //table or expression that returns a table
        FILTER(
                //table or expression returning a table
                Sales,
                //filter
                Sales[Country]="Germany"
        ),
        //expression
        Sales[Sales]
)

180. Conditional product
Modeling > new measurement

Total Product Tax =
PRODUCTX(

```
        //multiplies all values in a column that meet one
or more conditions
        //table
        'Country Tax',
        //expression
        'Country Tax'[Tax]
)
```

Glossary

ADDCOLUMNS (001,008,018)
ALL (030,031,033,034,036,037,043,044,050,088,095,..)
ALLEXCEPT (102)
ALLNOBLANKROW (044)
ALLSELECTED (089,098,099)
AND (024,034,073,077,080,096,100,116,117,122,135,..)
AVERAGE (005,006,007,008,169,178)
AVERAGEX (013,014,015,016,017,053)
BLANK (023,024,026,027,038,039,044,045,046,048,070,..)
CALCULATE (028,029,030,031,032,036,038,042,050,070,..)
CALCULATETABLE (006,009,010,052,053,060,080,087)
CALENDAR (001)
CEILING (067)
COALESCE (093)
COMBINEVALUES (103,161)
CONCATENATE (159)
CONCATENATEX (091,162)
CONTAINS (112)
CONTAINSROW (111)
CONTAINSSTRING (156,157)
CONTAINSSTRINGEXACT (158)
COUNT (034,045,105,106)
COUNTAX (107,108)
COUNTBLANK (046)
COUNTROWS (013,014,015,042,043,047,048,053,122)
COUNTX (037,109,110)
CROSSFILTER (038)
CURRENTGROUP (056)
DATE (170)
DATESBETWEEN (170)
DATESINPERIOD (171)
DISTINCT (003,004)
DISTINCTCOUNT (035,041,103,105,106)
DISTINCTCOUNTNOBLANK (038,039)
DIVIDE (127,164,165)

EARLIER (028,029,047,048)
EXACT (057,058,062)
EXCEPT (059,060)
FILTER (006,034,037,043,047,053,077,080,091,096,100,..)
FILTERS (084)
FIND (141)
FIRSTNONBLANKVALUE (130,134,135)
FLOOR (066)
FORMAT (001)
GROUPBY (056)
HASONEVALUE (070,071,088,089)
IF (023,024,026,027,048,081,088,089,090,091,113,115,..)
IFERROR (127,141,142,146,148)
IN (123)
INT (068)
INTERSECT (061)
ISBLANK (045,094,128,129,138)
ISINSCOPE (090)
LASTNONBLANK (132)
LASTNONBLANKVALUE (133,136,137)
LEFT (153)
LOOKUPVALUE (012,025,026,076)
LOWER (143)
MAX (101)
MAXX (013,014,015,053,075,167)
MID (145,146)
MIN (001)
MINX (013,014,015,052,168)
MONTH (001)
NOT (124,125,128,138)
OR (119)
PRODUCTX (180)
QUARTER (001)
RANKX (088,089,090)
RELATED (030,077,078,135,137)
RELATEDTABLE (016,017)
REPLACE (147,148,149,150,151)

RIGHT (152)
ROLLUP (005,006,007)
ROLLUPADDISSUBTOTAL (054)
ROLLUPGROUP (055)
ROUND (065,166)
ROUNDDOWN (064)
ROUNDUP (063)
ROW (019)
SAMPLE (079)
SEARCH (142,146,148)
SELECTCOLUMNS (011,012,016,017)
SELECTEDVALUE (072,093,094,169)
SUBSTITUTE (154)
SUM (011,012,013,018,027,030,048,050,052,069,070,..)
SUMMARIZE (005,006,039,040,050,074,084,086,162,..)
SUMMARIZECOLUMNS (013,014,015,054)
SUMX (056,077,179)
SWITCH (081,082,083,140,169)
TODAY (001,171,175,176)
TOPN (085,087,091,162)
TOTALMTD (173)
TOTALQTD (1734
TOTALYTD (175)
TREATAS (039,060)
TRUNC (069)
UPPER (144)
USERELATIONSHIP (092)
VALUES (020,021,059,060,091,104)
YEAR (001)

Printed in Great Britain
by Amazon